Second Edition

Greenman
and the Magic Forest

**Forest Fun
Activity Book A**

Susannah Reed

Contents

Welcome to Forest School!

Find and colour the animals in the forest. Draw you.

Look. Think about what is in the forest. Trace and draw.

I use my imagination.

Now you! Draw what you can see.

Look around you. Find these things and circle.

 I am creative.

 Now you! Make a window picture.

5

Trace the numbers. Count the leaves and match.

 I am clever.

 Make leaf prints.

Find five differences. Circle.

I care for the environment.

Now you! Make a forest broom.

Draw you. Draw a flower.

I feel calm.

Now you! Do some yoga.

Help the ants find the eggs.

 I am interested in things.

 Now you! Go outside and look at ants.

Find and trace the shapes. Colour.

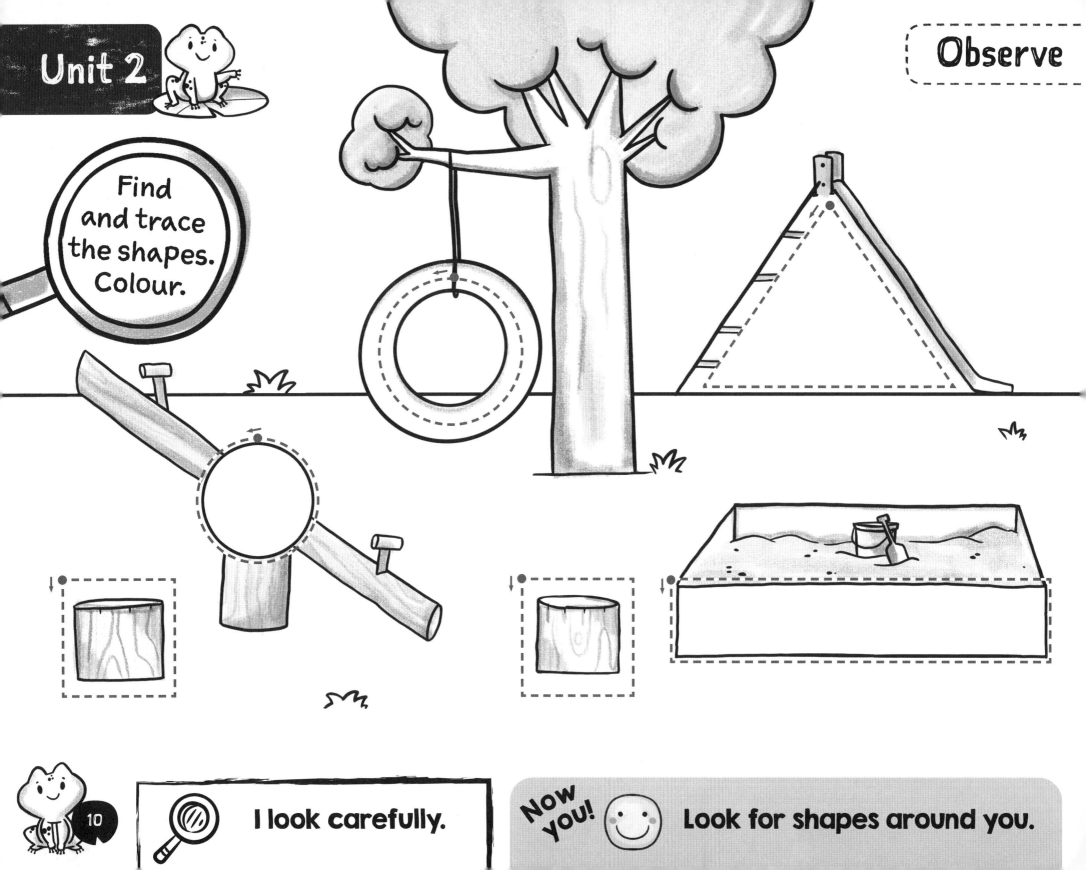

10

I look carefully.

Now you! Look for shapes around you.

Find and colour the animals in the forest.

 I have fun with my friends.

 Now you! **Play hide and seek.**

Follow and trace.

12

⭐ I am clever.

 Now You! Make a marble run.

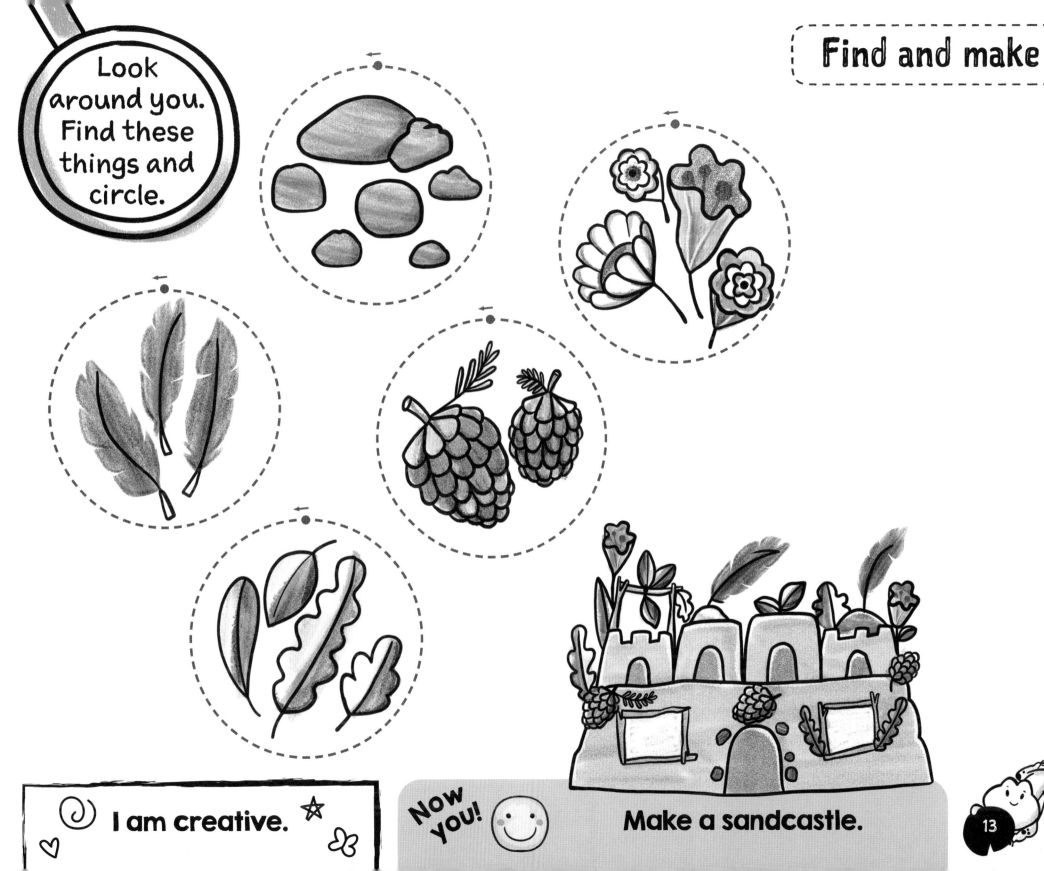

Look around you. Find these things and circle.

I am creative.

Now you! Make a sandcastle.

13

Look and trace. Colour the activities you like.

 I feel happy.

Now you! Do some exercise.

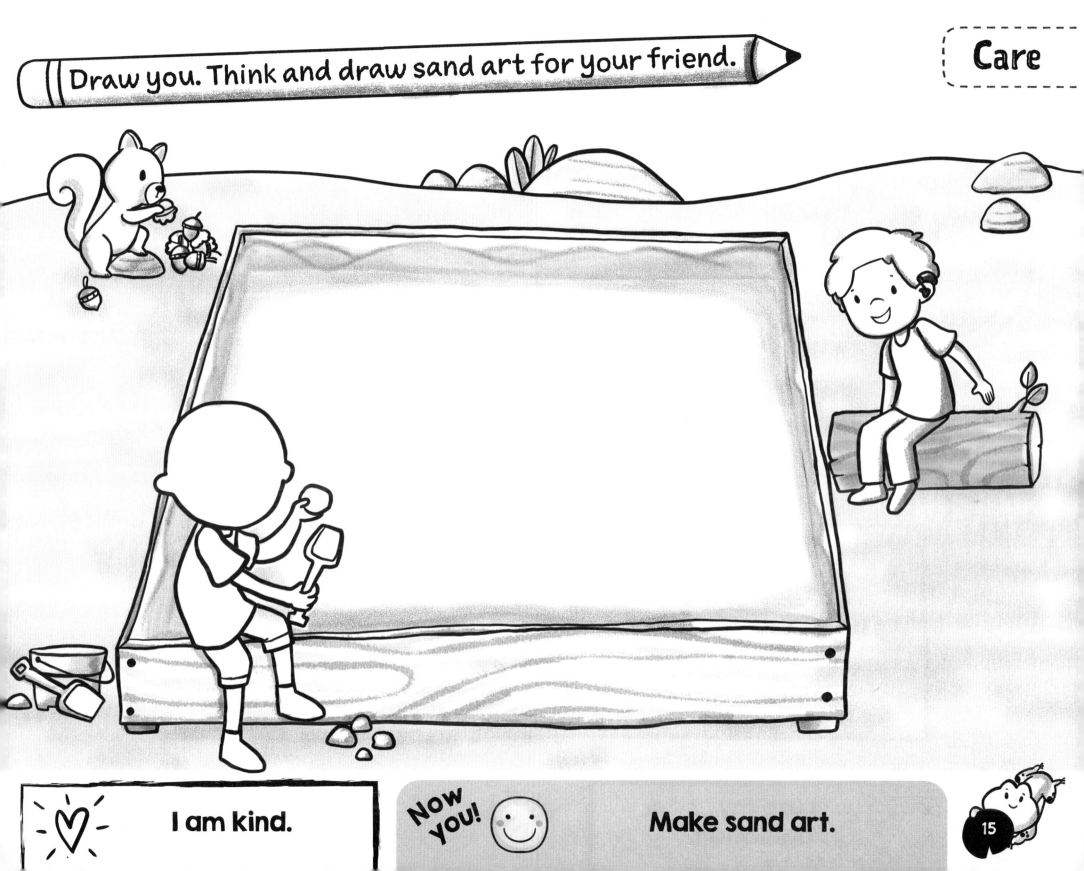

Draw you. Think and draw sand art for your friend.

I am kind.

Now you! Make sand art.

Look and match the pictures to the clouds.

I use my imagination.

Now you!

Look at the clouds.

Look around you. Find these things and circle.

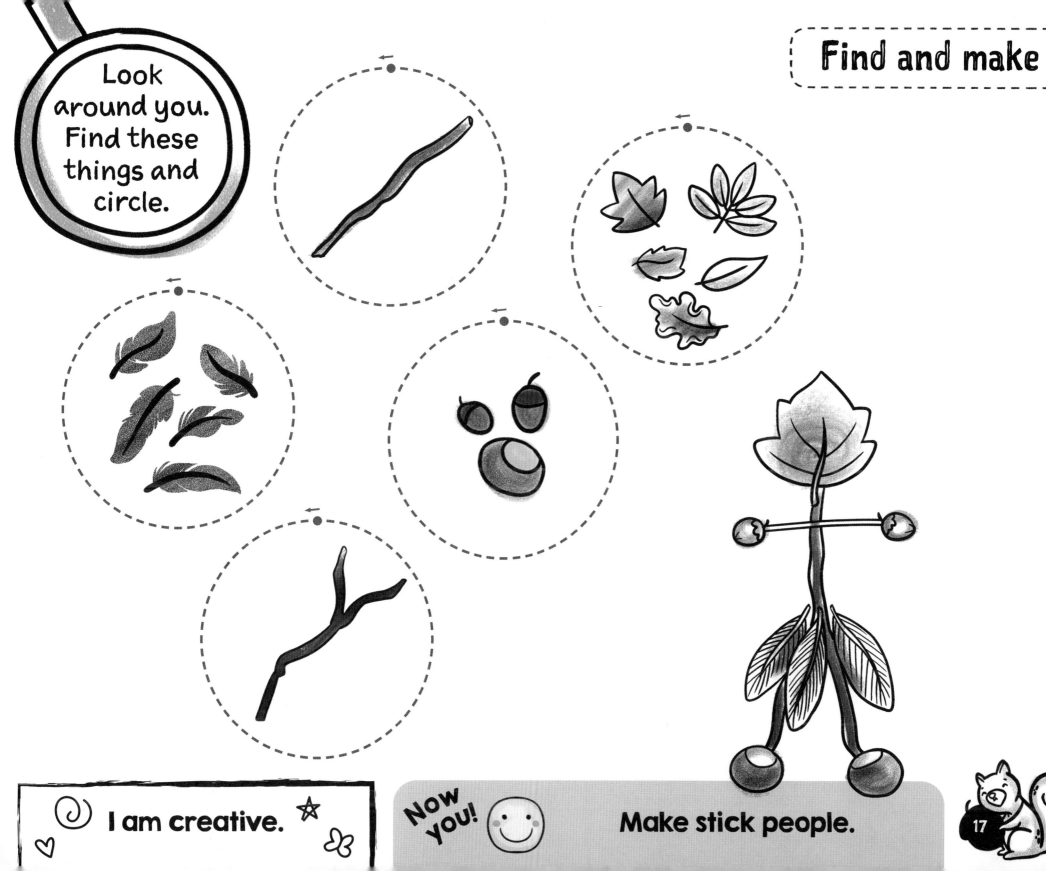

I am creative.

Now you! Make stick people.

17

Find five differences. Circle.

 I can do it.

 Make shadow pictures.

Trace the tree. Draw you.

I feel good.

Now you! Do some yoga.

19

Choose and colour. Look and colour the picture.

1

2

3

4

5

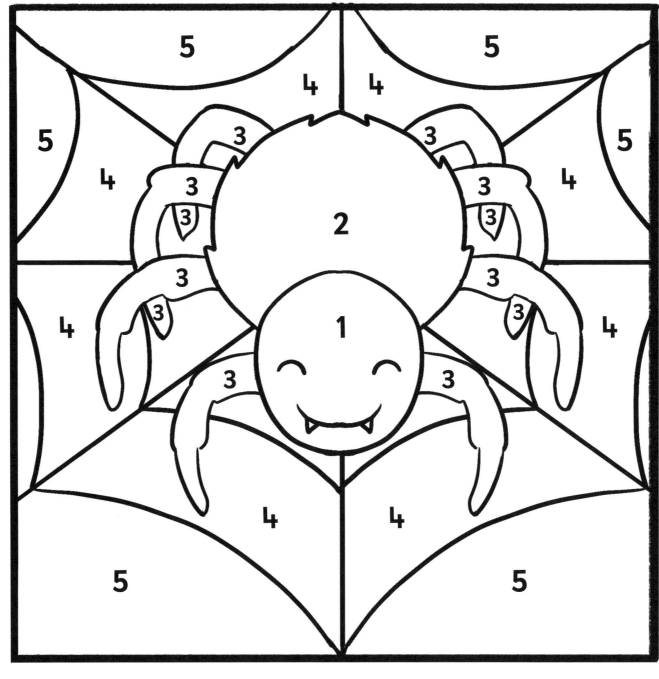

20

★ I try hard.

 Now you!

Find five insects.

Help the insect find the hotel.

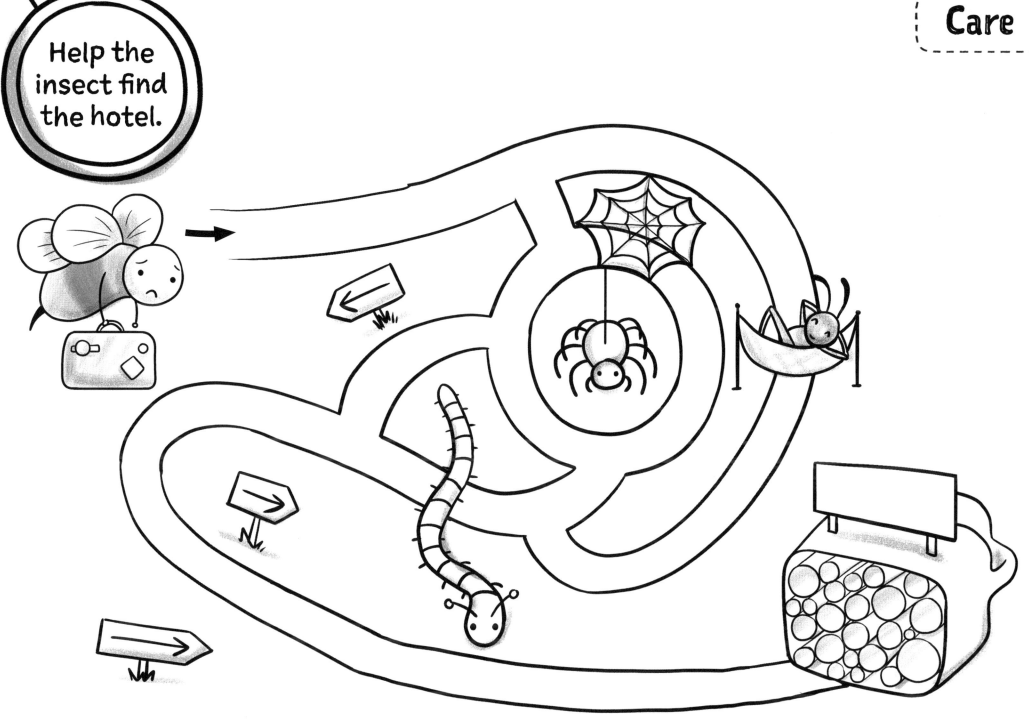

I care for animals.

Now you! Make an insect hotel.

Think and colour. Look and colour the clothes.

 I look carefully.

 Now you! Look for colours in nature.

Look around you. Find these things and circle.

I can do it.

Now you!

Make a nature hat.

23

Trace the puddles. Match.

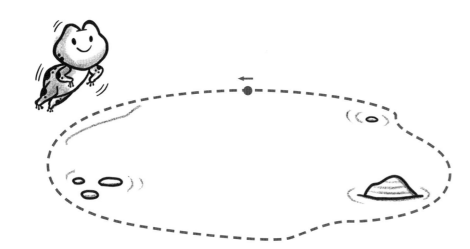

 **24**

I am interested in things.

 Now you!

Jump in puddles.

Look. Draw what's next.

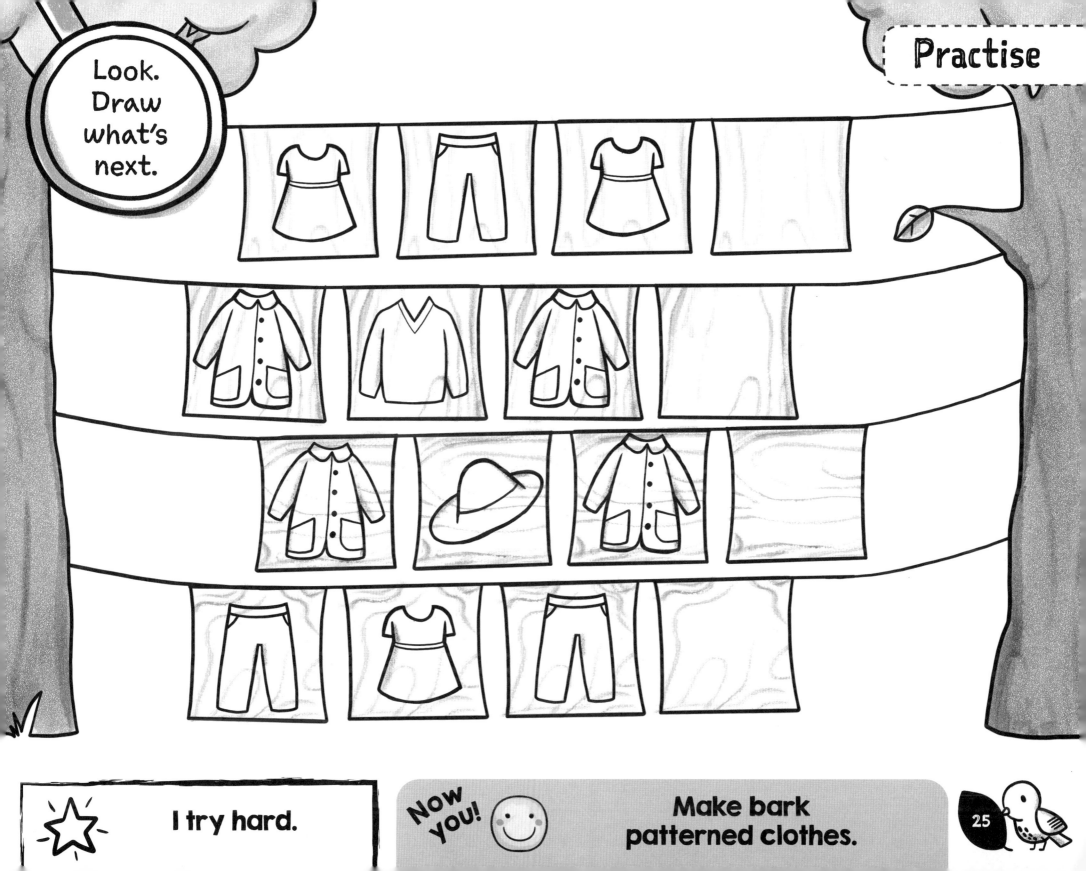

I try hard.

Now You! 😊

Make bark patterned clothes.

Find five differences. Circle.

I make good decisions.

 Now you! Put on clothes to play outside.

Think and draw.

 I have good ideas.

Now you! Reuse your old clothes.

Follow and colour the animals. Draw.

 **I look carefully.**

 **Find some footprints.**

Look around you. Find these things and circle.

I am creative.

Now you!

Make an animal.

Look and draw the animals on the bridges.

 30

I am clever.

 Make a strong bridge.

Circle what a cat can do. Colour the star.

I can do it.

Now you! Do some actions.

Trace and draw the butterflies. Draw you.

 **32**

 **I feel happy.**

NOW YOU! **Do some yoga.**

Think and draw an animal.

I care for animals.

 Now You! Be kind to an animal.

Find six differences. Circle.

34

⟳ **I use my imagination.** ☆ ♡ 🦋

Now you! ☺ **Make a forest kitchen.**

Look around you. Find these things and circle.

I can do it.

Now you!

Make a nest.

35

Follow and colour the sausages. Count the sausages and draw.

 36

I am helpful.

 Now you!

Cook outside.

Trace to match.

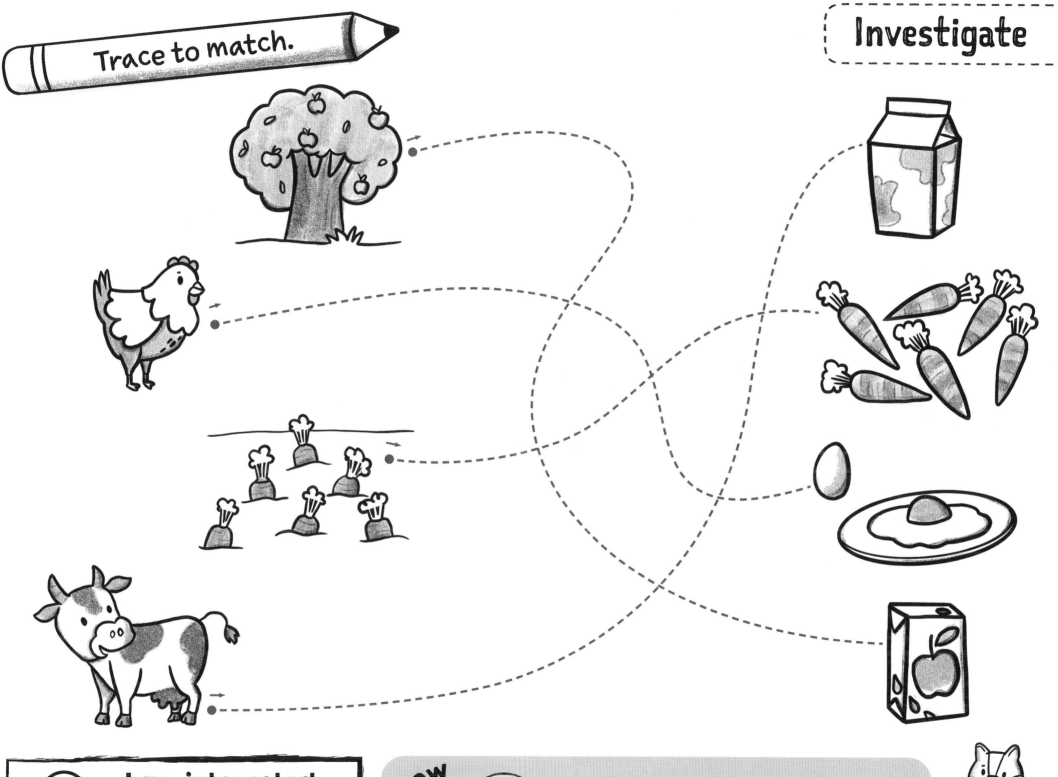

 I am interested in things.

 Now you!

Find out about food.

Count. Trace the numbers.

  +   =

 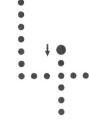 +   =

  +   =

 38

 I am clever.

 Now you! Plant some seeds.

Draw fruit. Think and colour the juice.

 I share with my friends.

 Now you! **Make fruit juice.**

CAMBRIDGE
UNIVERSITY PRESS & ASSESSMENT

Shaftesbury Road, Cambridge CB2 8EA, United Kingdom

One Liberty Plaza, 20th Floor, New York, NY 10006, USA

477 Williamstown Road, Port Melbourne, VIC 3207, Australia

314–321, 3rd Floor, Plot 3, Splendor Forum, Jasola District Centre, New Delhi – 110025, India

103 Penang Road, #05–06/07, Visioncrest Commercial, Singapore 238467

José Abascal, 56–1°, 28003 Madrid, Spain

Cambridge University Press & Assessment is a department of the University of Cambridge.

We share the University's mission to contribute to society through the pursuit of education, learning and research at the highest international levels of excellence.

www.cambridge.org
Information on this title: www.cambridge.org/9781009219679

© Cambridge University Press & Assessment 2023

First published 2015
Second edition 2023

20 19 18 17 16 15 14 13 12 11 10 9 8 7 6 5 4 3

Printed in Poland by Opolgraf

A catalogue record for this publication is available from the British Library

ISBN	978-10-0921-967-9	Activity Book
ISBN	978-10-0921-939-6	Pupil's Book with Pupil's Digital Pack
ISBN	978-10-0921-959-4	Teacher's Book with Teacher's Digital Pack
ISBN	978-10-0921-968-6	Teacher's Book Castellano with Teacher's Digital Pack
ISBN	978-10-0921-970-9	Big Book
ISBN	978-10-0921-969-3	Flashcards
ISBN	978-10-0921-960-0	Classroom Presentation Software
ISBN	978-10-0921-958-7	Pupil's Online Resources
ISBN	978-10-0921-942-6	Home Practice E-book
ISBN	978-10-0921-948-8	Puppet

Acknowledgements

The authors and publishers acknowledge the following sources of copyright material and are grateful for the permissions granted. While every effort has been made, it has not always been possible to identify the sources of all the material used, or to trace all copyright holders. If any omissions are brought to our notice, we will be happy to include the appropriate acknowledgements on reprinting and in the next update to the digital edition, as applicable.

Illustration

Sheila Cabeza de Vaca

Typesetting

Aphik, S.A. de C.V.